# ERNEST KANAK JR.

I0472789

# *The* WAY
# I SEE IT

A contemporary analysis of
the mess we call government—*with*
potential solutions

outskirtspress
DENVER, COLORADO

# Contents

# CHAPTER 1

# The Way I See It

Our political system is failing us. It is not bringing us the freedom and liberty that our Founding Fathers envisioned. Special interest groups dictate how things will be done. In the process, the little guy gets it shoved up his butt. Little guys always seem to lose. Is that right? No. Can it be improved? Let's hope so.

How are we going to fix our government and return to the people the knowledge that they once again may return to their freedoms and the American dream? It is my intention to stimulate discussion and solicit solutions by using my personal observations and reports gleaned from the public media to subjectively evaluate this nation's problems—big and small—and propose possible solutions. It seems that everybody complains about bad government, but nobody wants to do anything about it. It has been my experience that people who want change will almost never suggest ways to fix the problem, but they become very willing to comment and throw rocks at any and all proposed solutions to the problem. Well, this book is the first step in trying to fix the problems. Problems will be discussed and solutions proposed. Are all of these solutions the best ones? Probably not, but it is a start. Start collecting your rocks.

# CHAPTER 2

# How We Got to Where We Are

## Where We Started

Many of the people who came to this country as colonists were fleeing an artificial caste system due to birth and/or religious persecution.
Primitive conditions in the colonies made survival difficult. With the
difficulty surviving—and many did not—due to these conditions and
wars with the French and Indians, the survivors had to be resourceful
and independent. Later, after the colonies became more established,
the imposition of taxes by the British Crown caused many colonists to believe that they were being taxed without representation.
The culmination of the colonists' unrest resulted in the Declaration
of Independence and the Revolutionary War. The former colonists
became citizens of a new country—the United States of America.
The country's founders knew they needed a plan to govern, so they
wrote and accepted the Articles of Confederation. Unfortunately, the
Articles of Confederation were found lacking, so a Constitutional
Congress convened and the Constitution of the United States resulted. This document became the standard for the Rule of Law. The way
I see it, this document was written to protect the rights of minorities
and individuals who would not be protected in a pure democracy
where majority rules.

## The 1960s Changes

The changes to our country really accelerated during the 1960s. As one who lived during that period, I have observed three major changes that occurred in our society—one of them good and two that were bad. They were the civil rights movement, the attitude that everyone should look out for himself first, and drug usage.

Civil disobedience became very strong during this period with both the civil rights movement and the Viet Nam War protests. The civil rights movement's time had come and for a country that advocates equality for all, it was long overdue.

The other two movements were and are not as beneficial. The proclamation that everyone should satisfy their self interest before considering others has evolved into a "me first" attitude that emphasizes self and selfishness. Those with a huge ego most often have no respect for anyone else and their opinions and civility are dismissed. Ego triumphs over all. This attitude contributes to a breakdown in civil interactions between people and groups.

The third aspect of these changes was drug usage. Prior to the Viet Nam War, drugs were used by a very small portion of the population. It was generally accepted that the primary drug users were musicians. The Viet Nam war changed all this. Many young men who never used drugs were sent to fight in Viet Nam and came back to the United States addicted to illegal drugs. Until that time, wars were fought between well defined groups of men who dressed in uniforms. Viet Nam expanded the underground army concept that was used by the German occupation resistance groups during World War II. This made the whole country the battlefield and since many combatants were not wearing uniforms, it became very difficult to discern who the friends and enemy were. Presumably, this tactic introduced a tremendous amount of stress in the lives of those soldiers who were sent to fight the war and drug usage became a way to deal with the stress.

This might have been confined to Viet Nam were it not for the mass demonstrations against the war and the terrible treatment of the Viet Nam veterans after they had returned home to the United States.

## Federal Government

For approximately the last 100 years the federal government has played an ever-increasing role in the lives of ordinary citizens. Some of this change has been good and some has been bad. The rationale for this change has been that change is needed for the greater good, but in many instances the greater good costs the individual his personal freedom. From my perspective, I believe that all individuals should have the freedom to do what they want as long as exercising that freedom does not cause anyone else any harm. 'Live and let live.'

Since 9-11-2001, the federal government's intrusion into the lives of ordinary Americans has increased exponentially in the name of national security. The Bush administration consolidated several existing departments to create the Department of Homeland Security (DHS) with the goal of keeping us safe. We now know that the loser in this has been our individual constitutional rights--although some insist that those rights are still protected. The way I see it, those rights are not still protected and every new NSA disclosure reinforces that opinion.

The following is a list of news items reported in the public media that raise concerns about where our federal government is taking us. On some of these issues, there still may be many questions and no clear answer regarding how to fix it.

Detention centers---During World War II, the Japanese were rounded up in the name of national security and sent to detention camps. Since then FEMA (Federal Emergency Management Agency) and ICE (U.S. Immigration and Customs Enforcement) have established more than 900 detention centers. More recently in 2012 another 150 or more detention centers that require establishment in 72 hours were solicited.

Why are all of these detention centers needed? For whom are these centers to be used? Will the federal government ignore the Fourth Amendment again as they did for the Japanese during World War II?

Bullet proof guard shacks—the federal government has ordered bulletproof guard shacks. Why are they needed and at what locations will they be used?

The federal government has ordered thousands of armored vehicles similar to those used by our military in Iraq and Afghanistan. Why are they needed and who might they be protection against?

Why have the DHS personnel received military training?

Why do Social Security personnel now need to be armed? If you contend that they are not, then why did their department order 174,000 rounds of hollow point bullets?

In 2012 the federal government purchased about 1.5 billion hollow-point bullets—enough to shoot each person in the United States five times. The significance of this purchase is that the military normally uses full metal jacket bullets with the idea being that if you shoot someone, you remove from the conflict that person and two or three others helping him. Hollow point bullets are designed to go into a body the diameter of a pencil and come out the size of your fist. This is due to the expansion of the bullet in the body. These are not wounding bullets, they are killing bullets.

To use those detention centers, guard shacks and armored vehicles, the Federal government likely will try to establish martial law and suspend the United States Constitution. Martial law is dictatorship. To the best of my knowledge, the Congress has never contested the use of these executive orders and this President uses them almost weekly. This martial law action is one step away from setting up a dictatorship.

Martial law is a weak excuse to control the populace during civil unrest and is unnecessary because the Constitution established the militia. The founding fathers wisely specified that the militia maintain the peace. In our time this militia would be the unregulated militia— the 70 million plus armed citizenry who return to their civilian status once peace and law and order have been re-established.

In summation, what has happened in the last twelve years highlights many problems which could cause the end of this constitutional republic. Our Constitution defines the republic's rules for governance and how to keep it current using amendments. To me, it defines the term Rule of Law. Without the Rule of Law, we have anarchy. A pure democracy presumes all citizens to be equal with majority rule but makes no guarantee that minority rights will be respected. All elected representatives are supposed to represent the people since the people are the ultimate rulers. As someone who has lived many years and observed what has happened to this country, it is evident that our elected representatives no longer consider the people to be the rulers. The way I see it, it is time to fix the problem.

## Media

Many of these government actions were very briefly mentioned or never reported on by the so called main stream media (MSM). In other words, the MSM has failed the American public by adopting a biased agenda instead of remaining independent and safeguarding the public's interests.

During elections the media wants the power to control who is elected with an agenda that agrees with theirs, so they do not print extensive background checks of each and every candidate. What they do is wait until a few days prior to the election and print their endorsements. The problem is that the media is not supposed to have an agenda other than guaranteeing a fair and honest government.

In addition, in recent times, the media portion called the mainstream media has taken sides in the political battle between Republicans and Democrats. Not only have they taken sides, but by not reporting all the news and issuing propaganda reports under the guise of news, they have become propaganda ministers. It is unfortunate that voters must go to Internet blogger web sites to get the truth.

It is interesting to note that MSM television includes propaganda in their network programming and even the commercials aired. They must want to make sure the viewers do not miss their messaging.

The net result is that the average voter has a lot of help in staying dumb and uninformed. The liars' club is fully staffed with politicians and propaganda ministers who seek the power to control the use of government force.

What can be done about the propaganda press? The only thing they understand is money. As long as they can earn healthy profits and continue to issue propaganda, they will. For the printed media, the way to curb their propaganda is to not purchase their product. For the electronic media, those persons whose television has a telephone connection, your television viewer preferences are being monitored. The more viewers they have, the more they can charge for commercials. By not watching those shows and boycotting the show's advertisers, your message will be sent. For the free television market, only an advertiser boycott seems to have a chance to work.

## Politics

In today's world, politics is about the exchange of money for power and control. Should it be that way? I say no, but it is. Politicians say they need money to campaign for political office. Why do they need money? It is because the political districts are so large that they need to issue their political advocacy on television. In years past, politicians had to get out and meet the voters in the district so that he or she could tell them what his political message or program was. Unfortunately, today instead of broadcasting a political program, it appears that the only thing for which television is used is to smear the opponent. Truth, which should be a necessary requirement for anyone seeking political office, does not appear to be important. Is it any wonder that the current politicians are so terrible?

Since money is so important today, the aspiring or incumbent politician is always seeking contributions. Persons or organizations with a lot of money trade some of this money for political influence. How can a politician refuse any request made by his largest group of donors? It would be very difficult if this politician's only desire is to be re-elected. This gives the large donors more influence than a large group of small donors. This is why lobbyists with lots of money have so much influence on legislation. In today's political environment, this is why special interest minority groups have disproportionate influence over politicians. Money talks!!!

One would think that once the money has been raised it would be used to help someone get elected. What happens if there is any money left over after the election? You would think that it would be used for political purposes. That is not always the case. Elected officials use leftover monies for very expensive vacations, meetings and dinners. These funds are also used to employ family members for who-knows-what purpose. In other words, the use of contributions is abused. Some person who sends in a $25 check from his hard earned income because he wants to help the politician can be in reality helping the politician abuse his use of contributions. This is wrong and the current group of elected officials will never change it. Only an entirely new group campaigning for political reform can. Any politician who must smear his opponent during the election is one who cannot be trusted. If you want to try to trust your elected officials, you must not vote for any politician who uses smear tactics. If you do, the politician is telling you to bend over.

Smearing your opponent is a very effective way to make sure that good people never seek elective office. They do not want to have their families exposed to this abuse. Lack of financial connections is also another reason why good people do not seek elected office. The charlatans masquerading as politicians understand that and this is why, in general, the quality of politicians is so low. There are currently some elected officials whose priority is their constituents and good government, but they are very much in the minority. So sad!!

Much of the current petty political bickering is about winners and losers and which political party can force its agenda on the nation. Each of the two existing parties wants to have a presidential veto-proof majority in each house. Their agendas may or may not be in agreement with the majority of Americans. The United States is a pendulum nation and it swings from one extreme to another when it should stop in the middle. How can we try to stop these extreme swings? The way I see it, these extremist shifts would be more difficult if there was a third political party. A third party would require compromise on almost everything assuming that this third party was large enough and had enough unity. This third party could be comprised of many small two or three member groups. A third political party cannot mirror either the Republicans or Democrats or the system would not work. The two party system facilitates a totalitarian takeover of the political system and the country because it gives one party the power and control to use government force.

## Voter Fraud

In the 1960 presidential election, the state of Illinois was what today would be considered a swing state. The election between Richard Nixon and John F. Kennedy was a close one. The electorate in general was Republican downstate and Democratic in Chicago. On election night, as usual, the primarily Republican vote count was reported early. However, the Democratic vote count was delayed by Mayor Richard J. Daley. When the final vote count was reported, the number of statewide Democratic votes exceeded the Republican votes and the election was decided. The major mistake made by Richard Nixon was that he did not contest the election because it has been reported that he believed the country would not be served by doing so.

Based on more recent elections, voter fraud has become a way of life. When thousands of votes are counted and they all go to one candidate, when a voting machine does not record the selected candidate but his opponent and when on election day the number of voters exceeds the number of registered voters by more than 5%, common sense tells you that something is not right and voter fraud is a high probability. If America cannot have honest elections, we will lose our republic to the corrupt politicians.

Supposedly, voting machines have simplified and reduced the lines at the polls on election day. The problem with voting machines is that they can be very easily programmed to produce fraudulent results. Congressional testimony to the effect that changing two words of code will produce fraudulent results has done nothing to make elections more honest. Anecdotal evidence is that both Republicans and Democrats candidates have used the machines to fix election results.

Voter I.D. has been misrepresented as a way to discourage minority voting. Anyone who opposes voter identification also opposes honest elections.

When all these new voters show up at the polls on election day and want to vote despite not being registered, then they need to be photographed and fingerprinted prior to being given a ballot and a voter I.D. registration card. Should it later be determined that fraud has been committed, then upon conviction that person should spend a minimum of ten years in prison and be fined $10,000.

## The Uninformed Voter

The American voter has to be one of the most uninformed voters in the world. They ignore politics because it does not interest them or they don't like dirty politics. In fairness, it is difficult enough to earn a living without spending a lot time on politics—and I plead guilty on this account. How did I get there? Many years ago I listened to one incumbent presidential candidate who during the election called his opponent a war monger who wanted to start World War III. Well, the slander worked and after the election resulted in the incumbent returning to office, he then implemented about 80% of what his opponent who campaigned on the issues had recommended. The uninformed voters need to worry about a government selling them into a slavery of sorts and they would not even know it. People who trust their government are the stupidest of them all—guilty again, but I have reformed. It is sad to say that I have learned the hard way that no government entity can be trusted to do the right thing.

The Democratic and Republican parties know many voters are uninformed and exploit it to the hilt, but the Democratic Party has done a much better job of persuading the voters to vote for them. The voter has a lot of help to remain ignorant. Both political parties and the media do their best to keep the voter ignorant.

While each political party may vet their candidate, they appear to limit the release of information on the candidate's background. Why? The reason is that they want a candidate if elected to be indebted to the party and as such to do what the party wants. In other words, they want the power to control the elected official.

## Unions

Unions are one of the reasons that we have many of the benefits such as vacations, safer working conditions and higher wages that we all enjoy today, but unions are also one of the reasons we have local, state and federal government financial problems because politicians have made too many concessions to the unions in order to get union donations and support. Unions using their members' dues have bought many politicians using contributions to political campaigns.

Unions develop loyalty by protecting members from termination and promoting within the ranks based on union seniority. In general, when a job promotion is posted, the most senior union member bidding on the position will get it.

Unions are mini-dictatorships that are run by a ruling hierarchy who use strikes to seek concessions from companies in the industries they represent. Historically, the union membership has benefited from these strikes until the companies against which those strikes were held become insolvent. The reason these companies became insolvent is that their inept company management became so bad with too many concessions to the unions.

The union history has been marked with violence. Initially the violence was initiated by the companies that were dealing with the unions. Today, the perpetrators of this violence are the union members against those who oppose them.

With the move to increased mechanization in the coal industry during the last century, fewer union workers were needed. This wave continues today as high tech American industry uses more computer-programmed mechanical aids in an attempt to compete in the worldwide market against countries with much lower wage costs and poorer working conditions. The result is fewer people are required to produce each product.

## Politicians' Union

The politicians have created a de facto union. As long as uninformed voters re-elect politicians to office over and over, with each succeeding re-election, the de facto political union rewards that person with a more powerful and responsible position within the party. As we know, the political party with the most members controls the various committees within the Congress and appoints the committee chairmen. Committee chairmen are powerful persons because they control what legislation is considered. That person may be completely incompetent, but the more times he or she is re-elected, the more power he or she is given within the political party. Politicians are like clothes—they need to be changed frequently to stay clean.

## The Career Bureaucrat

Career bureaucrats have organized into unions. The union contracts with the government define what member rights and pay will be. These unions have morphed into political organizations which unfortunately have used union dues to support the political party that gives them the most. Both political parties have given away too much to these unions and the country has suffered and will suffer for generations. The current union favorite is the Democratic Party. Observation has shown that these unions are strong enough that when a union member makes a bad mistake, no matter how serious, there are no penalties. Remember these bureaucrats are the ones who write and issue the regulations that become law. Government unions are a threat to honest and fair government because like the de facto politicians' union, their loyalty is to their union---not their country.

The way I see it, we have gotten into this economic and political mess because we have professional politicians and career bureaucrats. Too many have been in office so long that they think that they are entitled to that position and act like they own it. They create and pass special provisions for themselves and their friends or the lobbyists' special interest groups. Since it has reached the point that running for office requires a lot of campaign money, the special interest lobbyists have purchased too much influence in our political system and in some cases may "own" elected officials.

Several recent events have demonstrated the need to test bureaucrats for competency before they are appointed.

Prior to the Madoff Ponzi scheme scandal, an accountant with competency in accounting and finance was advising the regulators that something was wrong, but he was ignored. The reason he was ignored is that the regulators were lawyers who obviously knew nothing about finance and accounting. The public was defrauded of billions of dollars because the people charged with protecting them were incompetent in that field. Just being an attorney means nothing if there is no competency in the field to be regulated. Once the Ponzi scheme was uncovered, Madoff was convicted and sent to jail.

Another example is the Obamacare rollout. After three years and spending more than a reported 500 million dollars, the Obamacare website was a complete disaster. As of December 21, 2013, the website that was to be up and running as of October 1, 2013 did not do the job it was supposed to do. It remains to be seen if anyone will be terminated and/or go to jail because of this mess, but based on past history it would not be a surprise if the group who messed it up were not promoted. The Peter Principle is alive and well in the federal government bureaucracy.

The professional politicians and career bureaucrats have created an out-of-control monster where competency does not seem to matter and corruption reigns supreme.

## The Professional Politician

1) When professional politicians make a mistake, they will make excuses to blame something or someone else. They almost never pay the price and take responsibility for their actions.

2) When asked a question they don't want to answer, they will accuse others of racism, prejudice, injuring children, killing seniors,

etc. Alternately, they will talk around the question and never answer it. They use emotional responses---never the facts.

3) They lie and don't tell the truth.

4) If the truth becomes known and it does not favor the professional politicians, they will go back and repeat steps 2 and 3 again.

5) They talk fairness and practice deceit.

6) A professional politician has only one constituent---herself or himself. Their main objective is to get re-elected.

7) Their loyalty is to their political party--not to the voters—because their party standing determines how much power they can wield.

# CHAPTER 3

# Major Issues of the Day

## Second Amendment to the Constitution

FBI statistics have been reported that crime has gone down since the year 2000. This has happened despite the fact that there are more people in the United States and more guns per capita. The second amendment states: "A well regulated Militia, being necessary to the security of a free State, the right of the people to keep and bear Arms shall not be infringed." The only reason for gun control is to disarm the people so that an armed group can forcibly overthrow the government of the United States. This is the true reason for disarmament. For that reason, our Founding Fathers created militias for the express purpose of suppressing any domestic insurrection. The militia's role is today poorly defined on purpose, but rest assured that every law abiding citizen of this country with a firearm should be prepared to defend this country as a member of the unregulated militia against all invaders—foreign and domestic. Every man who possesses a firearm is automatically a member of the unregulated militia. In light of today's military, I would include women in this group. The unregulated militia's role is to suppress any insurrection—like a forcible government takeover by the military--and once law and order is restored, go back to being civilians again. Federal executive orders try to take over this militia role, but the military would be trying to enforce an unlawful order which would contradict their oath to uphold the constitution. I would estimate the size of the unregulated militia to be more than 70 million people.

The Western movies and shows typically revolved around a sheriff or marshal enforcing the law. When someone broke the law and fled, the sheriff would round up a posse to go find the lawbreaker and bring him back so that he could be tried for his crime. What the posse was in reality was the unregulated militia. When the criminal was caught and returned for trial, the posse disbanded and the members resumed their civilian lives just as members of the unregulated militia would do.

As recently as 1946 a group of military veterans in Tennessee organized a militia group to recover an election ballot box that had been unlawfully removed by the local sheriff. The local sheriff wanted to fix the election so he won whether he had enough votes or not. The ballot box was retrieved by the militia and the crooked sheriff was ousted from office.

The unregulated militia is all that might one day stand between us and a totalitarian takeover.

The unregulated militia is also one reason no foreign country could ever conquer and occupy the United States. All negative talk about the militia is propaganda directed to disarm the American public.

## The Economy

The current administration has increased the national debt by 5 trillion dollars in five years. This debt was incurred based on the pretext that more government spending would help people find jobs. What seems to be missing in this assumption is that government produces nothing, but it does consume monies by taxation, reducing the available capital to produce marketplace goods and services to sell. It is the old guns or butter argument. The net result is that there are fewer persons working as a percentage of the total workforce than any time in the last thirty years. Millions have given up looking for work. What have we gotten for the new 5 trillion dollars of debt? "Another day older and deeper in debt" to quote an old Tennessee Ernie Ford song.

Many of the historical and economic theories were developed when the world's population was agrarian with small businesses and very little science and technology in existence. When a farmer or small business person needed help, it was very easy to hire extra help to meet an increased demand. This is no longer possible when positions require someone with expertise that it takes years to learn and develop. It would seem that the increased technology and rapidly changing economies make trying to control any economy very difficult.

Government-managed economies are complete disasters because it is impossible for any group of professional politicians and career bureaucrats to effectively manage an economy with millions of participants-- each with his own idea of what he thinks is best for him. The Union of Soviet Socialist Republics (USSR) had total and complete control of their citizens and their economy. Did it work? No!! Why?? Their system demonstrated that when you expect little from your citizens, that is what you get. One of the precepts of Communism advocates that everyone should "receive according to need and produce according to ability." People are people and to expect someone to do another's work without compensation is stupid. It just doesn't work!!

It would appear that those in government who do not worry about the nation's debt are those who believe that the debt will never be repaid or are of the opinion that inflation will increase to the point that repayment will be much easier. Failure to repay means bankruptcy and high inflation means that the dollar is worth much less and its purchasing power will diminish. In either case, if a dollar cannot be used to purchase goods and services, some other means must be used. That typically means that gold and silver become the only acceptable payment. Barter also becomes a way to get what is needed.

Do we as a country want to have to use metal coins and barter to meet our personal needs? I think not!

Those politicians in power will protect themselves as they always do and the ordinary citizen will pay the highest cost. This is unacceptable.

Based on who the professional politicians and career bureaucrats are, it is unrealistic to expect them to want, pass and live with a balanced budget. A Balanced Budget Amendment to the Constitution is impossible with the current congressional, executive and judicial office occupants.

This nation's deficit spending must be stopped. To ensure that the nation's integrity and honor are preserved, this nation must begin to pay down its debt using balanced and surplus federal budgets.

## The Tax System

Death and taxes—the only certainty in our lives. But how much taxation is fair? To the socialist, very high tax rates are good as long as the socialist doesn't have to pay them and he gets to spend the tax monies. For normal people, all taxes, although recognized as necessary, are too high.

The tax system in this country is based on catering to special interests of one sort or another. It seems as though favoritism has the largest impact on what tax rate is charged. The losers are the rest of us.

The federal IRS scandal discussed later is a prime example of the abuse of power to use government force. This power is given to the IRS because they enforce the rules they write through regulation. The power to grant exemptions are a regulator's dream and the reason we have corruption. Congress plays a big part in the corruption game by making special interest exemptions or modifications to the tax code. This must be changed. Instead of thousands of pages of tax code, we should have one that consists of maybe no more than ten typewritten pages of code. If we have a flat tax of say 15-18 percent of income with no allowable exemptions, then there will be no interpretations needed. This new tax code should be written in plain English instead of legal form which would only give attorneys about a thousand reasons to file a lawsuit. After a few years the tax rate could be changed to meet the country's needs.

Another way to raise taxes is the value added tax which pays a tax every time an item for purchase is handled by someone until it finally reaches the consumer. This is a more complicated way to collect taxes and it does not inform the consumer as to how much tax is included in the product.

The fairest way is to have a federal sales tax. Some people would argue that this kind of tax unfairly penalizes the poor. These same people are the ones who advocate for welfare, unlimited unemployment insurance benefits, Medicaid, food stamps, etc. THERE ARE NO FREE LUNCHES. EVERYTHING COSTS MONEY AND SOMEONE MUST PAY. THERE MUST BE AN INCENTIVE FOR EVERYONE TO CONTRIBUTE AND IF SOMEONE NEEDS MORE, THEY NEED TO WORK FOR IT.

## Free Markets

The way I see it, free markets are the economic model that uses freedom of choice. What other system would allow a twenty something entrepreneur to become a billionaire? The answer is no other economic system. The free market system allows someone with an idea to develop that idea and profit from it. It has been labeled as a greedy system because it conforms to human nature; i.e., if I work hard and am successful, then I will be rewarded for my efforts.

It is really interesting to observe the phenomenon of people who use the free market system to create huge fortunes and then become philanthropists and political socialists. Have they forgotten that some forms of socialism endeavor to eliminate private property?

It is also interesting to note that many rich people only want to relinquish their fortunes after they die. Do they do this because 'with great wealth comes great individual freedom?' Rich people have much more individual freedom to do what they want than does the ordinary working man or woman.

## Planned Economies and Political Systems

Socialism, communism and totalitarianism are all economic and political systems that exercise total control using government force and cause a loss of individual freedom. Loss of individual freedom is what makes these systems unworkable. Note that all of these systems try to breed out individual freedom, but it never works because the idea of doing what you want is ingrained in people. In the animal world, it is all about survival.

It is very hard to understand how a planned economy can effectively work because it is impossible for any group of people to have enough information and knowledge to micro-manage the lives of hundreds of millions of people. Planned economies try to micro-manage the lives of everyone. When they create a job to employ someone without a need for that service, the only thing they do is spend tax money for busy work. No goods are produced by government and if the service provided is just a duplication of what is already done, then the total efficiency of the service task is lowered. This is a waste of time, money and human resources.

Planned economies historically have had chronic unemployment. Just look at the high unemployment numbers for the European Union. Unfortunately, the U.S. federal government through over-regulation and deficit spending is trying to duplicate the European model.

Socialism and Communism are government-run economic systems that reward mediocrity and laziness. These systems take from the well-to-do and redistribute their wealth to the less fortunate. By doing this, these systems destroy the incentive to work hard by informing everyone that if you work hard, your reward will be to lose your hard earned gains to the state so that the state can reward the so-called unfortunate. Someone needs to tell them that their systems are contrary to human nature, but they will not listen because running such a system gives those directing the system tremendous power to control the people using government force.

Scarcity is one result of Communism. This is why a man buys several loaves of bread when there is enough bread at home because when he goes by the bakery there is no line. This is why someone who has lived under Communism says that if they put the Communists in charge of the Sahara desert, after five years there would be a shortage of sand.

My observation is that good economic systems attract workers and poor economic systems have the workers fleeing.

## The Decline of the Middle Class

The U.S. Census Bureau has reported that the median household income has been declining since 2008. In years past, there has been much written on how the U.S. economy was shifting from an industrial to a service economy. Based on past history, this translates into high paying industrial jobs becoming lower paid service industry jobs, and from jobs requiring an industrial skill into jobs requiring a sales skill. Historically, service industry lower level jobs have always paid less.

The unions share a good part of the blame for why there are fewer industrial jobs in the United States. Prolonged strikes are effective because they can completely shut down a company. If the company is not financially strong enough to withstand a prolonged strike, the management must give in to the union demands. Of course, the result is that the company product cost must be raised in order to pay the workers and still make enough profit to stay in business. Since we now live in a global economy, when the product costs get too high, the company's choice is to either go out of business or try to relocate to another place where they can make a profit. If there are federal government regulations that must be met and the company wants to stay in business, they must relocate to somewhere outside of the United States. It is a vicious cycle and common sense does not prevail. Oops, there go the good paying jobs.

## Publicly Owned Corporations

Over the past 100 years, companies have evolved from private companies to publicly owned corporations with both good and bad results. In years past, entrepreneurs created the companies that grew into many of the huge corporations we all know. At that time, these entrepreneurs who became Chief Executive Officers (CEO) owned all or most of the stock when they incorporated. The boards of directors were most likely selected by the CEO. The CEO who owned a large percentage of stock shares had a vested interest in increasing the value of his stock. If the CEO demanded a high salary, it really didn't make much of a difference because he owned so much stock. When some of these companies became so large that they controlled much of the country's economy, anti-trust laws were passed and the companies were broken into smaller companies to promote competition.

In today's world, many of the current company CEOs own little or no stock. They are given options to purchase stock at reduced prices but may not exercise those options. Many boards of directors who are tasked with protecting shareholder interests will allow the CEO to run the company like he owned it. They do this because one of the conditions for their serving on the board is that they must be provided with an insurance policy that essentially makes them immune from lawsuits for not protecting the shareholders' interest. In other words, the corporate governance organization is broken.

How do we fix it? The CEO and other corporate officers must own corporate stock equal to 5-20 per cent of their annual salary. This creates an incentive for the CEO to increase stock value which is to the shareholders' benefit and supposedly is the corporation's main objective. The boards of directors which have too frequently become rubber stamps for the CEO, must also be compensated in company stock. Meeting attendance would be expensed by cash payments. Both the company officers and members of the board of directors would not be allowed to sell their stock as long as they served. Any additional stock purchases above these minimums could be bought and sold like any other stock purchase.

The rationale that companies must be huge to compete against government run companies has been sold to the American public. For energy companies, in the days when the world's energy supply was controlled by a few countries, maybe it made some sense. With the advent of new energy technology, this may no longer be true. Extremely large companies exert too much influence on the economy and the effects of mismanagement can have disastrous effects on a country's economy. Like the banks, no company should be too large to fail. Once again, the socialist political system prefers few large companies as opposed to many smaller companies because it is easier to control fewer companies. All of this leads to restraint of trade and price fixing--sometimes with government collusion. This is bad for both the consumer and the country. In this country, it has been documented that most of the new jobs are created by small companies. A vibrant economy generates many new companies and jobs. A socialist type government stifles this job creation in an effort to control the economy with disastrous results most times. The European economic model has demonstrated that socialist run governments breed stagnant economic growth with high unemployment. Unemployment is an indicator of under-utilization of human resources. At the present time, the American economy is duplicating the European model.

## Banks

Break them up into many smaller banks. It is much easier for a political system to control a few large banks than it is many much smaller banks. Too big to fail stinks along with banks handling both investments and traditional bank functions. Banks should serve the public by lending money to support individual as well as industrial and commercial banking needs. Banks involved in investments lead to stock market manipulations. The banks along with the government interference in the home mortgage market created the 2008 economic meltdown. Issuing mortgages due to government intervention to people that had no way to repay the loan should have sent some people to jail as was the case during the earlier savings and loan scandal. To date, I am not aware of any participant in the latest mortgage meltdown going to jail. Governmental administration of banks is bad. Government should be insuring that the banks are kept safe and secure.

The Federal Reserve policy of buying the bonds issued by our overspending government troubles me. We are generating debt that may never be repaid for generations. Interest rates are artificially kept low to reduce the government's debt service payments to a minimum while at the same time this tactic severely penalizes the citizen who has spent a lifetime saving for retirement. It is not fair!!! And while they say they do, government doesn't care if it is not fair.

At the same time the bank discount rate (interest rate) that banks pay the Federal Reserve to borrow money is 0.75 per cent. They then charge the consumer 12-20 per cent interest on their credit card balances. To me, this is usury. The banks who contributed to the 2008 economic meltdown as mentioned previously are making lots of money with this practice. It is called "money for nothing" to quote a song. Anecdotal reports claim that the reason these credit card interest rates are so high is that the banks will issue a credit card to your dog. Why should the consumer have to pay for this lending malpractice? Who has been sent to jail?

It is interesting to note that a former United States senator/state governor was the head of an investment firm that "lost" and cannot account for a billion dollars. Has anyone been charged with any crime for this? To date and to the best of my knowledge, the answer is no. This example illustrates that if any ordinary working man or woman loses money, they are fired and/or charged for a crime; however, if a rich and influential person "loses" a billion dollars, no one is charged with anything. Money talks. And the abuse of the system for those with access to large amounts of money should be criminal.

## Terrorism

Terrorism is something Americans have lived with especially after 9/11/2001. It was not the first time Muslims killed someone here in the United States in the name of Islam and it will not been the last time. How can we protect ourselves from this terrorism? Since the Fort Hood massacre demonstrated that even trusted and U.S. born Muslims can become terrorists, it would seem that the only way to protect yourself is to treat every Muslim as a terrorist. In a way this does not seem fair because all Muslims are not terrorists, but there are only one or two Muslims in this country publicly condemning this terrorist behavior. The vast majority of Muslims in this country by their silence approve of terrorism. When the peaceful Muslims unite to support the secular state and start to pursue and prosecute terrorists in their midst, then we can start to consider evaluating our attitude toward Muslims. Until then, if it ever comes, BEWARE!!!!

Another way to fight terrorism is to stop all immigration from Muslim countries except for those persons who in the past have supported American soldiers on the battlefield. Those persons put their lives in jeopardy by helping Americans. To continue to allow people into this country whose religion advocates killing non-Muslims would be stupid. This prohibition must also include those Muslims on student visas.

What attracts some to Islam? The way I see it, one reason is that men are supreme. To a Muslim man, women and children are property for him to do with as he wants. His religion allows him lie to and kill non-Muslims. He can kill some family members with no consequences using Sharia law. For an uneducated man, Islam makes him feel and act superior. The losers are the women and children.

May I suggest that if the Muslim countries want to live in the 15$^{th}$ century by practicing Sharia law, obviously they can do so. In the 15$^{th}$ century, there were no airplanes and autos, no electricity and computers, so when these countries return to the 15$^{th}$ century lifestyle, they will no longer have any use for these modern items. It would then be expected that most commerce with the West would disappear and when the Muslim world infrastructure starts to deteriorate, it would only be replaced with new technology from Muslim sources. Of course, the European Union and China will not agree to this, but then let them deal with jihad.

## United Nations

In 1945 the United Nations was created to promote world peace and harmony among nations. When North Korea invaded South Korea in June 1950, the UN voted to assist South Korea and a multinational army of UN troops fought on behalf of South Korea to keep it free.

In October 1950 China invaded the nation of Tibet and nothing was done.

In 1990 when Iraq invaded Kuwait, the UN tried to use sanctions to get a negotiated withdrawal of Iraqi troops. When this failed, another multinational army was used to drive Saddam Hussein's Iraqi troops out of Kuwait.

Since then, the systematic extermination of Christians or genocide has spread its ugly tentacles in Africa and the Middle East. Thousands of people have been killed and continue to be killed and the best the UN can do is issue sanctions. They might send UN troops into a country after the killing has stopped.

The UN is now trying to convert the United States into a poorer country using Agenda 21 under the direction of a UN world government. This program has already been started by the current administration using sustainability as the agenda. Basically Agenda 21 advocates that affluent people are a problem because they consume too much of the earth's resources, insists that any animal has the same rights as a human being, restricts where people can live to high rise communities in concentrated areas, insists that there is no private property and individual freedom, dictates that consumption of natural resources must be limited and a select group of people using totalitarian control will tell the masses how to live their lives. Obviously, gun control is a necessity because if the populace has a means to defend themselves, how can total government control be achieved?

The UN's leadership wants to reduce the United States to third world status using Agenda 21. The UN is a corrupt organization from which the United States must withdraw, stop all funding and give the UN two years to relocate their headquarters to another part of the world.

## Defense

The Defense Department is one of the largest expenditures the federal government makes. To some, too much money is spent on defense and not enough on social programs—the traditional economic tradeoff between guns and butter. What seems to be forgotten is that without a good defense system, the freedom our forefathers and many veterans have died to provide will be lost.

With the elimination of the draft and the conversion to an all volunteer military, the pay has increased substantially--which is good. What is bad is that it eliminated the need to serve our country. Without military service, the patriotism that comes with service is lost. Everyone at some time in their life should perform service to our country. Universal military training with no exemptions for a year would be a good way for everyone to serve their country. Those who would object to military duty could perform a year in a non-military role.

As the military has become smaller and smaller, the general staff level officer corps does not. This does not seem right. Do we really need all these generals, admirals, etc. for the size military we have now? Do all of these staff level officers contribute to bloated defense budgets and waste or has the Congress forced the military to spend excessively? This needs to be investigated from a scientific basis instead of a political basis. It should be noted that promotions to the level of general are political appointments. To become a general, admiral, etc., the person must be a good politician. We have too many professional politicians now—we don't need more in the military.

Military procurement is over budget many times. This is due to the changes that are made after the contract is issued to the contractor. This also means that the design was not properly defined prior to issuing the contracts. If the design is really new and innovative, then the design changes must be done during the research phases of the project when the costs are controlled because there are only one or two prototypes. The only design changes that should be made after the contract is issued should be when the contract design will not work. When this happens, then the research and development done was inadequate.

One of the reasons the American military has done so well is new technology. New technology is the way we stay ahead of any potential adversaries. Even with defense budget cuts, it is absolutely necessary that the technological research continue.

## NSA Spying

The IRS scandal was followed by the revelations leaked by Edward Snowden that NSA is monitoring and recording millions of American phone calls, emails and financial records with blanket FISA (Foreign

Intelligence Surveillance Act) approval in violation of the Fourth Amendment of the Constitution. Search engines and companies such as Microsoft, Google, Verizon and others have been reported to have assisted NSA in this spying. It has been reported that Microsoft has gone so far as to give the NSA spies their unencrypted Outlook messages. A FISA court which rules on what kind of surveillance can be done has become an administration rubber stamp for all that is not constitutional in the pretext of national security.

The military personnel who work for NSA took an oath to follow and protect the constitution, but it is clear that they have disregarded their oath and the constitution, using the excuse that it is necessary to protect the country. NSA employees have become outlaws and must be prosecuted and dealt with as outlaws. When convicted, as outlaws normally are, they go to jail. Instead of jailing the outlaws, it would not surprise me if this administration promoted the outlaws.

It should be noted that the NSA spying did nothing to prevent the Boston Marathon bombings. Human intelligence should have prevented this if the federal government was not so inept. This human intelligence was supplied by Russia and was ignored by the one or more federal bureaucratic organizations. How can these organizations say they earned their salaries by ignoring these warnings? Sadly, they did not earn their salaries and more people died.

According to published reports after 9-11, the government concluded that the reason 9-11 happened was that the U.S. government was lacking an effective human intelligence network to provide warning. This was supposedly built up and it was human intelligence that located Osama Bin Laden. Unfortunately, it appears that the current administration that used this information to find and kill Osama Bin Laden is slowly destroying the network that has been built and prefers to spy on U.S. citizens. This must stop.

## Immigration

Illegal immigration is once again rearing its ugly head here in the United States. The Immigration and Reform and Control Act of 1986 proved that giving amnesty to Illegal aliens did not work because the promise to secure our borders was never implemented. Instead our corrupt politicians have pandered to special interest groups and have ignored the problem. They just don't care about this human problem. They also have, in my humble opinion, broken the law by failing to enforce the existing laws.

That makes the last two presidents outlaws who should be tried, and if convicted, sent to jail for not doing their sworn duties to enforce the law as constitutionally required.

Instead of 3 million illegal immigrants, we now have from 12-20 million illegal immigrants. To grant amnesty again will almost guarantee that there will soon be 20-40 million illegal immigrants. We as a country cannot grant amnesty. The Democratic Party wants amnesty because they expect to use entitlements to get all the new citizens to vote Democrat. In other words, the new citizens are for sale. Are they though? I don't know.

Many illegal immigrants work in the cash economy. They pay their bills and collect their pay in cash. None of this income is reported and no taxes are paid. They do use government services such as Medicaid. When they do use a fake social security number, they may or may not file a tax return. When some have filed income tax returns, they reported many dependents and, in one case, many returns were filed at one address and millions of dollars were sent to that one address. Why did not the government discover this problem before millions of dollars were refunded? Does anyone in Washington care about potential fraud? It sure does not look like it.

We cannot once again grant amnesty to persons who have broken the law. Most of the illegal immigrants are reportedly seeking work. Fine. Let us once again have a guest worker program such as the former Bracero program but without the abuse that happened then. During that time, there was guest worker abuse. If contracts to work must be signed, then these contracts must be in both English and the worker's native language. The wage must be agreed upon and enforced. The company or farmer that uses these guest workers registers them in E-Verify and assumes responsibility for their whereabouts. If the guest worker runs away, the employer must inform the authorities and the reluctant worker found, arrested and deported. That worker then goes into a database that precludes him or her from ever participating in the program again.

A properly run program should dramatically reduce the number of undocumented immigrants trying to infiltrate the United States borders. During the peak Bracero years, there were more than 400,000 guest workers per year.

With legal status, the 12-20 million workers would have to register and make themselves known. Citizenship could only be gained by serving in the armed forces (this has been done for decades) and following normal citizenship requirements. Normally the application would be made in the country of origin, but I am sure since they are here, some fair adjustment could be made. They need to go to the back of the citizenship line.

Birth citizenship for any child born in the United States would apply only if one of the parents is a verified United States citizen. Pregnant illegal immigrant women sneaking across the border to have their child born here would stop. Once it made sense for children born here to automatically be citizens, but not anymore, especially in this entitlement society.

The laws already exist for persons who overstay their visas. Now the DHS has no idea where those who overstay their visas are. This must be changed so that they can be found and deported to their home country. Is it going to take a terrorist attack to finally get this law enforced? The federal government hires thousands of people to enforce a health care law that most citizens do not want and lets potential terrorists stay here. Does that make sense?

There can be abuse of the immigration process. This is especially true of potential immigrants with a skill set wanted and needed by American companies. To reduce costs, the company will specify worker requirements in such a way that an unemployed qualified American cannot meet the need and the lower paid foreign worker can be admitted.

With these reforms, only terrorists and drug dealers would not be allowed to cross our borders. Therefore, under these circumstances, anyone illegally crossing the border becomes an invader and should be shot in defense of the border. When the bleeding hearts start complaining, I suggest we make them work at the border to enforce illegal immigration. The persons currently working on illegal immigration and drug enforcement do the best they can without always having the staff and equipment needed. Double fences do work!!!! Only corrupt politicians do not work.

## Welfare

Welfare is both a godsend and a cancer on our society. It helps provide a minimal subsistence to keep people alive while at the same time it can destroy all incentive for individuals to improve their lives through hard work and education. Education is included in this analysis because it is the vehicle that allows individuals to greatly improve their standard of living. Manual labor is an honorable and good way to earn a living, but it becomes more and more difficult as one becomes older. History has proven that when most of the populace was doing manual labor of one sort or another, the human beings' lifespan was much shorter.

Public housing is a prime example of welfare gone bad. In Chicago, Illinois the government built multistory housing units called Cabrini Green. These units were supposed to furnish decent housing for the poor. When they were new, they probably accomplished that goal, but after some years, the units became used and rundown. Did the tenants abuse the housing or did the government fail to adequately maintain the units or both? I don't know, but I do know that these units eventually became crime-ridden places to live. The units continued to deteriorate until more recently they were torn down. So much for the government furnishing housing units for the poor.

The way I see it, everyone here on earth should have a reason to be living. If all a person does is lie around doing nothing, why are they alive? What purpose do they serve in helping themselves and society? Should not we have a society whereby one person working to improve his or her standard of living inadvertently improves someone else's life by producing something or providing a service? A job done well makes the person who does the work feel good about themselves. Work accomplishes this no matter how small and trivial the work seems to anyone else. To create a system that rewards sloth and irresponsible procreation is a disservice to everyone.

For hundreds of years, people have donated their time and money to charities that have helped the poor and disadvantaged. They do it—not as a job—but in the interests of helping someone in need, and usually the help is delivered without demanding anything from the recipient. When we make it a job to help those in need, we create a government bureaucracy that uses taxpayer money to control the recipient of the help. If government has no demands on the person receiving help, then the system borders on anarchy. Perhaps the best way to deal with chronic welfare is to limit the duration during which one can receive welfare benefits similarly to the way unemployment is administered. Currently, after many years of welfare benefits, the welfare recipient becomes an indentured servant to the state and potentially a political party.

# CHAPTER 4

# Entitlements and Healthcare with the First Steps Toward Their Resolution

## Social Security

One of the reasons for our debt liability is entitlements. *To those who paid into a social security system that was supposed to invest those funds in a retirement account, social security is not an entitlement but a return on their mandatory investment.*

All participants must be able to select another way to secure their retirement instead of the existing social security fund. Existing law has a 457 Plan which is a social security alternative. Participants contribute 7.5% of their wage on a pre-tax basis to their account which is invested in a guaranteed annuity with a guaranteed minimum rate of return. Since this account is 100% vested, should the participant pass before age 65, the beneficiaries receive the account balance. Social Security's death benefit is $255. With a 457 Plan type of account, the younger people will be able to, along with their IRA and 401k accounts, be in control of their future retirement. This will be difficult to implement because this plan would decrease the amount of taxes sent to Washington to be wasted by them and I do not expect them to willingly give up the control of such a large amount of money. A phased introduction could gradually make the transition from a government plan to a private plan. The young people may have to resort to civil disobedience demonstrations to get it.

Many older people only recently have been able to have a pre-tax IRA and pre-tax 401k, so they were not given the opportunity to save for their future. This means that their payments must come from the existing taxes or the general fund.

## Structured Benefit Plans vs. IRA-401k Plans

For many years companies have offered their employees structured pension plans when the employee retired. Usually these plans defined when the employee was eligible to retire and what the monthly benefit would be. Some companies also offered paid health plans for retirees. Due to government regulations on how much money the company had to have in reserve to guarantee that the monies would be there when the employee retired, companies learned that those monies exceeded what they could reasonably provide, so the 401k system was born.

The advantage with 401ks for retirement plans is that employees are offered company sponsored investment plans to increase the value of the account. Hopefully the companies will offer conservative investments like mutual funds that actually increase in value each year. These plans are separate from the Individual Retirement Accounts (IRA) that are individually initiated and funded. The advantage for the 401k plans over a structured pension plan begins when the employee retires and rolls over his 401k into his IRA. Structured pension plans pay a fixed benefit which does not increase to keep up with inflation, but IRA's can be invested in stocks, bonds and mutual funds. Wise investing in the IRA can help the retiree keep up with inflation while at the same time receiving retirement income from the account.

## Medicare

Medicare's financial problems are well known. Medicare pays about 80% of the patient's cost, so a supplemental health insurance policy is a must. Presently, a Medicare patient with a supplemental insurance policy pays little or nothing for doctor's visits and medical procedures. If a medical procedure or visit is not covered by Medicare, the supplemental insurance pays nothing. To save money, the routine doctor's visits probably should be paid for by the patient and no reports sent to Medicare and/or their Medicare supplement insurer. When the patient pays the total bill and no records are sent to Medicare or the supplemental insurance company, this saves the cost of paperwork for the doctor, Medicare and any insurance company. Since most Medicare patients do not have a lot of money, any procedure that costs more than say $100 would be covered by Medicare and private insurance. What all patients need is protection against catastrophic health costs. If the government and the healthcare providers got out of handling the paperwork and billing for routine medical visits costing less than $100, the money the government spends on Medicare and its enforcement should decline.

## Medicaid

Medicaid was started to help the poor with their health needs. It should not be expected to pay for every patient's medical services unconditionally. Since anyone who shows up at an emergency room is guaranteed treatment by federal law, the Medicaid system is ripe for abuse and fraud. The system can and is abused by couples who have children, but do not marry. A low income woman will most likely meet the Medicaid income requirements by not reporting her partner's income, so the state will pay for her medical needs. Why should a patient go to a doctor and pay for his treatment when he can go to the emergency room and get free treatment? This type of abuse must be stopped.

There should be a minimum payment of $20 for every time someone shows up at an emergency room. After say five visits per year, for each additional visit, the required payment should increase.

# Healthcare

Everyone today worries about healthcare—either you have it or you don't have any and you worry about getting sick. If you have insurance, past history has shown that it is becoming more and more expensive and you worry about how you can afford to insure your family. If you are in your 20s and in good health, you probably don't worry about healthcare at all.

Until World War II, health insurance was the individual's responsibility. Whether or not you had insurance was a personal decision. During WW II with wages frozen, companies started offering medical insurance as a benefit in lieu of higher wages. This approach allowed employers to deduct insurance costs as a business expense and insurance companies to reduce their adverse selection costs by increasing the pool of insured. When only people in poor health are the ones seeking insurance protection, this causes the insurance premiums to become quite high and is called adverse selection. The larger the company, the lower should be the cost per insured to a certain point and the larger pool of insured should reduce the underwriting risk to insure the pool.

When people made a career of staying with one company for thirty or more years, an underwriting history was established by the insurance companies. When people started changing jobs, new employees became unknown risks for the new company's insurance carrier. This introduced the previous health condition exemption. In the past, for the new employee, there would be an exclusion for that previous condition for a number of years---usually two years. Any medical issue related to that previous condition would not be covered for the specified time period. With Obamacare, previous health conditions no longer can be excluded from the insurance policy. This is one of the Obamacare provisions that the insurance buying public likes and the provision that increases the health insurance premium.

Most people have agreed to share their medical history with a medical insurance bureau when they apply for a health insurance policy. This information goes into a file on each person in broad coded terms which then can be used by member insurance companies to underwrite the health insurance risk for that person; however, this information is not intended to be used by an underwriter to declare the person uninsurable. In other words, each person's rights and privacy should be protected.

One of the reasons that health insurance has become more expensive each year is because of government mandates. A bureaucrat in the state capital working for an insurance commission is convinced that a certain feature should be required for all insurance policies issued in the state and convinces the commissioners to make it mandatory for ALL policies. This makes the insurance company include a premium for this mandatory coverage in everyone's policy whether it is needed or not. Normally when someone applies for an insurance policy, the application and any physical examination results are sent to underwriting where the insurance company's financial risk is determined. For group insurance policies, there is no physical examination so adverse selection is factored into the group policy premiums. When everyone must be insured for a mandatory risk, then the insurance company will assume some percentage of applicants have serious problems and determine the premium increase based on this percentage. This practice leads to higher insurance premiums for everyone.

Another reason for increased health costs is the progress modern medicine has made in keeping people alive. As more and more ways are found to keep people alive that twenty-five years ago would have likely died, the costs for these procedures and subsequent treatment have led to increased medical costs. As more procedures are needed to keep an individual alive, that person's lifetime medical costs must increase. The insurance industry has recognized this by reducing the cost of life insurance and increasing the cost for medical and disability insurance. The emphasis for an individual now is disability. With the progress medicine has made, more and more people survive medical procedures and the person, if unable to work, goes on disability. Perhaps this is one of the reasons more and more persons are requesting social security disability benefits, but it is equally probable that when someone has a health problem, they choose to seek disability instead of changing their way to earn a living as was the case years ago. For example, many years ago when you had a back problem, you sought to find employment in a job that did not require a strong back. For some young people today, that change in job choice is no longer considered as an option. They have been entitled to rewards since birth and, to them, entitlement is a way of life.

To control costs, the consumer must be the one deciding what insurance coverage he, she or the family needs---no one else. This can happen only if the insured owns the policy and not his employer. Changing jobs is no longer a problem when the insured owns the policy. At the same time, the health insurance tax deduction used by the company must be changed to an individual/family tax deduction. If the insurance company thinks that a certain type of coverage is needed and the insured does not, then the insured must sign a waiver to document that the coverage was offered by the insurance company and declined by the insured. The insured takes responsibility for his insurance needs and suffers the consequences if wrong.

With everyone buying their own insurance policy, the insurance company will use all available data from the medical insurance bureau to underwrite the risk. To avoid adverse selection, individuals must be allowed to band together into much larger nonprofit cooperative groups and have these groups negotiate a group premium. This way helps both the consumer and the insurance company and seeks to avoid the high premiums that adverse selection dictates. In addition, the state insurance commissions must stop issuing mandates and allow their citizens to request a quote that meets their needs. Another way to reduce insurance premiums is to stop restricting the companies that are allowed to provide insurance coverage in each state and encourage interstate competition. If individuals seek to have insurance that covers only catastrophic events, they should be allowed to do so.

One of the best insurance programs in the past has been the Health Savings Account (HSA) in conjunction with a high deductible insurance policy. A percentage of the insured's income is deposited into the HSA account on a tax free basis. This allows the insured to purchase a high deductible insurance policy and pay for minor insurance needs using the HSA funds until the deductible is met. Monies not used are kept in the account and are carried over for future use.

It should be noted that currently some states provide insurance coverage for those people who are deemed uninsurable and cannot buy health insurance due to an existing health problem. The premiums are two or three times higher than normal, but at least insurance coverage is available. The way I see it, it would be a much better use of taxpayer monies if the state helps those uninsurable citizens pay their higher health insurance premiums instead of assuming the liability of the medical treatment cost.

In some states, doctors have paid $250,000 per year and more for malpractice insurance. Doctors who have dedicated many years to gain their M.D. and specialty should not have to spend exorbitant amounts of money on insurance. Tort reform is a must for these states. At the same time, these doctors must not support those doctors that should not be trusted to practice medicine.

To avoid the Obamacare healthcare insurance penalties imposed on companies with more than 50 full time employees (defined as 30 hours per week), companies have started hiring only part-time (29 hours or less per week) employees. This strategy allows small companies to stay under the 50 employee limit. However, fewer hours means lower income. For low wage workers, this means that they must work two jobs with no overtime pay to make the money they may have previously made working only a single job. When Obamacare becomes too complicated to implement and enforce, then an excuse to simplify and go to a single payer healthcare system will have been born. Why would the federal government want to run the healthcare system? The answer is to increase the federal political power and control over its citizens using government force.

# CHAPTER 5

# What Legislatures Need to Do

## The Legislative Branch

After a law has been passed by the legislative branch and the executive department (president, governor, mayor, etc.) signs off their concurrence, it is the executive department's responsibility to enforce the new law. The problem arises when the legislature does a poor job of writing the law and has the executive department produce additional clarifications called regulations. If the legislature is going to pass a law, it is imperative that they retain responsibility for the law and hire the necessary staff to finish all parts of the law and regulations prior to issuing it to the executive department for enforcement. Congressional oversight has not worked in preventing executive department over-regulation. Letting the executive department write regulations is a huge mistake. It empowers the executive department to both make and enforce the laws. I sincerely doubt the founding fathers would agree with this.

## Congressional Oversight

As mentioned previously, congressional oversight of legislation does not work. When the Congress lets the career bureaucrats in the executive department issue regulations that are supposed to support the legislative purpose, they lose control and the separation of power is reduced. Under current law, after the Congress discovers that the regulations do not agree with the law's intent, they can have hearings to discuss the regulations and must by joint resolution within 60 days agree that the new regulation is null and void. To revisit a law that may have been passed years earlier is an inefficient way to conduct the country's business. The Congress must complete the legislation by writing the regulations and then issue in parts or the complete package to the executive department for enforcement. This will require that the Congressional staff be expanded to fulfill this task and should reduce executive staff. Overturning a proposed regulation when it is written by Congressional staff should be an internal change. It would then put the burden of making the regulation null and void on the executive department. If the executive department wants to nullify a regulation, then since the law has already received executive approval, a simple congressional majority will overrule the executive decision and the regulation will become law. The executive department of government is there to enforce the laws, not make laws through regulation.

## The Budget Process

The way that most governmental organizations budget and request funds directly contributes to constant spending increases. Each department develops and submits a budget for approval. This budget is approved--possibly with adjustments--and then given to the department to spend for that fiscal year. Assume that one department will not have spent all of their budget for that fiscal year which will end soon. What this department will do is dramatically increase spending to ensure that all the budgeted funds are spent. Why? These funds will be spent not because of need but because if they do not spend all the funds, they may not be able to ask for an increase in next year's budget. Are more funds really needed for that department? Sometimes yes and many times no. Maybe this department requires only four people, but they have a budget that can support five. So they will hire someone only to make sure that year's budget is spent. That new person may have little to do because only four people are needed.

Is this wisely spending the taxpayers' money? Obviously the answer is no, but this is how government abuses the taxpayer. Another way budgets are abused is by awarding employee bonuses for doing their job. What needs to be done is to not spend the money. It should be returned to the government or into a rainy day fund. Instead of moronic appropriations policy, we need government officials that will use good judgment and common sense. Since these budgets are prepared by bureaucrats whose job is dependent on the budget, they have a vested interest in predicting that more money is needed. There is no incentive to spend money wisely and frugally.

As long as the department's objectives are met and the public is served as needed, maybe an employee incentive system which rewards departments for keeping expenses down and meeting department goals would work better. People being people means that there must be a personal incentive for them to want to excel.

Another player in this budget process is the elected official. The public has entrusted elected officials with the responsibility to use their money wisely. The official must determine whether or not the departments are doing what is necessary for them to do and in the most efficient manner; i.e. not wasting the taxpayer's money. Bloated budgets and waste result when the elected official fails to do his job. Too often in the past, these officials have not taken responsibility and, unfortunately, continue to be re-elected. In this case, it would appear that the voters don't really care how high their taxes are or they would pay more attention.

# CHAPTER 6

# The Executive Branch Needs to Follow the Constitution

## The Executive Branch

The executive department currently has the responsibility to enforce the laws passed and issue regulations. Unfortunately, some executive departments decide that they will not enforce a particular law or part of a law. It is the responsibility of the executive department to enforce the law. If you don't like a law or part of one, change the law. That is the rule of law. To not enforce the law moves the government closer to anarchy and the way I see it, it is breaking the law; i.e. the person not enforcing the law is an outlaw. Outlaws must be prosecuted and, if found guilty, sent to jail. It should be noted that the last two presidents have failed to enforce existing laws—both of whom are Ivy League law school graduates.

## IRS Scandal

The IRS has targeted those conservative organizations seeking 501(c)(4) approval. In addition, the IRS targeted pro-Israel and religious organizations. Any organization that opposed the administration was targeted. The rank and file IRS union employees have demonstrated that they are in lock step with the administration and have been rewarded for this behavior with promotions and bonuses and no punishment for these corrupt practices. The IRS is a cesspool that must be abolished in favor of a tax system where potential government corruption is removed.

## ATF Fast and Furious

Who authorized the ATF to allow almost 2000 guns purchased in the United States to be sent to Mexico for use by the Mexican drug cartels? Congress tried to find the answer to this but the Attorney General initially lied about his knowledge of the case and President Obama has exercised executive privilege to effectively shut down any investigation of this scandal. What happened to the most transparent administration in history? Did it ever exist?

## Benghazi

Four Americans died when terrorists attacked the embassy in Benghazi. No help was sent to save these Americans and the Obama administration has refused to say who issued the order to stand-down (not assist those under attack at the embassy). Then the administration lied by publicly stating that a movie caused the incident and terrorists were not involved.

The President promised that the persons responsible for the death of four brave Americans would be found and brought to justice. One year later nothing has been done. As usual, the employee union protects its members even when they may have participated in a crime by covering up what really happened.

State Department whistleblowers who have testified to Congress about Benghazi have been penalized and those who have not talked are being rewarded with promotions.

The way I see it, the State Department is as corrupt as the IRS and many changes need to be made.

## James Rosen Case

The Attorney General lied to a Federal judge to be able to monitor all of Mr. Rosen's phone and email communication as well as those of his parents.

## Associated Press Case

Here the Department of "Justice" tapped the phone lines of many AP reporters and editors in an attempt to find out who in the government had leaked information to AP about a terrorist plot. The net effect of this action was that whistleblowers now refuse to talk to AP reporters-- which is what the government wanted.

# CHAPTER 7

# The Judiciary and the Legal System are a Mess

## The Judicial Branch

The way I see it, the Constitution has federal judges appointed for life to ensure that they are immune from political influence. It hasn't worked. Today, all federal judge appointments are political. This practice has created an allegiance to political parties and an agenda instead of protecting the rights of the people. By approving the Affordable Care Act, the Supreme Court demonstrated that the five justices who voted for the act are in fact political hacks who should be impeached.

When the judicial branch of government is asked to rule on a law and the Constitution is followed, it is as it must be. Unfortunately, there are judges as previously mentioned who do not strictly follow the rule of law and decide to in effect create new law under the pretext of a "Living Constitution." For local and state governments, these judges can be removed by an election. The only way federal judges can be forced from office is impeachment and the Congress has done a terrible job in policing the federal bench and removing judges who are political and do not follow the Constitution and the rule of law. Since Congress has failed so miserably in this task, maybe it is time for federal judges to be elected. If they are going to be political, let them periodically face the election process.

## Criminals and Babies

Today we have millions of our citizens incarcerated in our prisons.

The persons today in prisons have lost their freedom for crimes against society. Many of these persons are habitual criminals who have committed many crimes. As punishment, they lose their freedom but are given a place to sleep, three meals a day and medical care that may not be available to many ordinary citizens. The incarceration of these persons costs the state many millions of dollars. Habitual criminals are in and out of prison many times. Shouldn't something be done to persons who choose to be criminals and spend many years in prison? Some criminals commit horrific crimes against humanity and are sentenced to life in prison without parole. Juries continue to sentence criminals to life without parole.

My question is why must the taxpayer support and pay for those persons who refuse to obey the law or are programmed to die in prison. What is gained by keeping them alive?

It must be mentioned that abortion is a form of the population control advocated by the United Nations Agenda 21 and that this policy has been in force for several decades in China. There the practice has been to abort only female babies so sons would be born. Now the country has millions of twenty something males with no females and I suspect that the Chinese government is worried about a potential insurrection. Maybe this is why they have relaxed their one baby policy.

On the other hand, women who decide after becoming pregnant that they do not want to bear that child can get an abortion. In a way, it makes sense to abort a baby that the woman does not want if she will not raise that child to become a productive citizen. Many unwanted children become wards of the state and later wind up committing a crime and are sent to prison. If the woman does not want the child, maybe an early abortion is the right solution.

My question is why do we provide humane incarceration for career criminals and those who commit horrific crimes against society and then kill babies that are innocent? What does it say about a society and a judicial system that protects criminals while killing innocent babies?

## Tort Reform

Attorneys charge by an hourly rate and have no budget and no schedule. It seems greedy to charge clients excessive percentages of a settlement as a fee in addition to charging by the hour. For large settlements, it is possible for one case to make the attorney a millionaire.

To reduce the court backlog, prosecutors and plaintiff attorneys instituted plea bargains. As long as justice is served, they are good; but there are instances especially when a guilty party accepts immunity to testify against a potentially innocent defendant where this tactic may cause more harm than good. Some countries limit this practice to those cases where the punishment for a conviction is five years or less. This forces the really serious crimes to trial. Maybe this tactic should be considered here.

Due to the cost of trial litigation, many people and organizations use the threat of a lawsuit to extort concessions from a potential plaintiff. This tactic has consistently been used by fringe groups to receive concessions from government entities which most likely do not have any taxpayer budget to fight lawsuits. Is this justice and has the public been served? The way I see it, the answer is no.

The way I see it, most lawsuits exist to make the attorney money—not to seek justice for the plaintiff. Why did the plaintiff hire an attorney? Because the way the system currently works, no one wanted to listen to the plaintiff's complaint unless an attorney was involved. Another broken system.

This same tactic has been used by persons who threaten to file a lawsuit over an insurance settlement. In this case the fault probably lies with both parties. The insurance companies will refuse to negotiate with the injured party unless that party hires an attorney. While it would seem that in most cases the injured party only wants to be restored, the insurance company will refuse to reach a fair settlement and an attorney enters the picture. The winners are the attorneys and the losers are the injured parties and the insurance companies. Is this justice? Once again, the answer is no.

Since trial lawyers contribute large sums of money to political campaigns, the system will be difficult to change with present elected officials. Tort reform has been successful in some states and should be implemented in all of the states. It places dollar limits on specific types of lawsuits in order to provide justice without exorbitant legal and settlement costs.

# CHAPTER 8

# Other Important Issues of the Day

## Education

The federal government involvement with education began in the 1950s. At that time the comment was made that with the introduction of federal monies there would be federal control. This prediction has become fact. The losers have been the children in our schools who are indoctrinated instead of educated.

When young school children are instructed to sing the praises of the current president, the politics have become more important than the education. If the federal government starts educating four-year-olds on the pretext of helping their education, they will be teaching them that the state is all important and their parents are not as important as the state. They will have the kids tattling on their parents just like Hitler had the German children doing. We do not need this.

The only true way to educate the children is to return total control of education to the local government. With individual school districts deciding what the curriculum should be, the diversity the Feds seem to so covet should be restored. Local school districts should decide what materials should be used to teach reading, writing and arithmetic. True American history must be taught and not the revisionist history currently being taught. The federal government is using the schools to indoctrinate the children with socialist propaganda and teaching them to follow orders—not to reason and think.

It is constantly stated that more monies must be spent on education. The quality of education does not correlate with its cost per student. While education costs have continued to go up, the quality as confirmed by test scores have gone down. Diversity and affirmative action have lowered standards. Instead of tutoring those in need to meet the standard, the system was dumbed down—it was made easier. How can this nation compete internationally with a poorly educated populace?

One of the reasons cost per student has gone up is that we have too many administrators. Why do we need a principal for each high school grade and an overall principal? It is a waste of money. The money should be spent on the curriculum and teachers in the classroom instead of more administrators. If the administrator needs more money, maybe that person should consider changing jobs and getting out of education.

The way I see it, the teachers unions are interested in more pay and benefits--not the education of the children. Educating the children comes in a poor second.

Why are we frequently hearing news reports of teachers having sex with their students? What has happened to the morals of our teacher population? Is it too late to hope to return to the past teacher standards?

The school systems have eliminated recess and gym classes and then complain about overweight children. Why do school lunches have to be multiple choice meals? Is this necessary or can this be simplified by offering one meal choice per day. If the parents and child do not want to eat what is offered, then send a lunch to school with the child. Why are vending machines with soft drinks and snacks in any K-12 school? Is it about the money? The school system eliminates exercise and then complains about overweight children. The schools offer multiple meal choices for lunch and then complain about poor nutrition instead of offering a 'take it or leave it' nutritious lunch. This situation reminds me of an Albert Einstein quote: "The difference between stupidity and genius is that genius has its limits."

The common propaganda today is that everyone must go to college to get a good job. This is total B.S. Not everyone wants to or should go to college. Do you think that your plumber or air conditioning repairman went to college? No! Was it necessary for that person to go to college? No! Can they earn a good living? Yes! It should be noted that once they have gained enough experience many of these persons can become entrepreneurs and own their own companies.

What has happened is that federal guarantees have made loans available for a college education and student debt is approaching one trillion dollars. Are all of these degrees in areas where there are jobs? Once again, no! Who has been counseling these students in career choice? Does it make sense to borrow a lot of money for a job which has salaries that are so low that it will be difficult to repay the loan? The answer is obvious. The government has sold everyone on the baloney that a college education is a must-have, and to support this, the federal government has taken over the student loan program which in 2013 has produced a profit of 41 billion dollars while total student debt has increased.

When a career choice makes a college education a necessity, what is wrong with living at home and going to a community college for the first two years? The answer is nothing. In many cases the instruction at a community college will be in smaller classes with more individual attention than in the university classroom with 50-60 students and taught by a graduate student instead of the professor. It should be noted the community college teachers are professionals who are there to teach, not to do research and publish papers that for many university professors is how they are evaluated. Research is an important part of the university, but not to the undergraduate student trying to learn and get a degree.

Many young people starting out in college may not know for sure what career they really want. If this evaluation period is done at a four year university, and the career choice is changed, it will increase the education cost significantly because it costs more to attend a four-year school with room and board than to attend a community college. Only when cost is not a consideration should a student attend a four-year university and then keep changing their field of study toward a degree.

## The Environment

The Environmental Protection Agency (EPA) was created in December 1970 after Rachel Carson wrote her book "Silent Spring" about what damage DDT was doing to wildlife and the environment. At that time, this book demonstrated the need for environmental regulation. Scientific evidence has shown that DDT clearly affected wildlife such as the American eagle. Since this pesticide use was stopped, the eagle has made a recovery. To continue to be able to use pesticides without long term ill effects, the chemical industry has learned how to manufacture biodegradable pesticides.

During the recent federal government shutdown, only essential workers were required to continue working. What is the federal government trying to tell us when it classified over 90% of the EPA staff as non-essential? My question is, do we really need all the regulations being generated by the non-essential EPA staff?

## Transformation of the Automobile

After the 1970s oil embargo, the Department of Transportation and the EPA began to set automobile Corporate Average Fuel Economy (CAFÉ) fuel mileage standards which have caused our cars to become smaller and more fuel efficient to reduce our foreign oil needs. It made sense in the 1960s and 1970s to conserve fuel because those large cars were inefficient and got poor gas mileage. At the same time, the government started dictating how cars should be built and operated. Soon there were regulations on bumpers, seat belts, catalytic mufflers, air emissions, fuel ingredients such as lead and ethanol, etc. With each change or mandate, the cars became smaller, more fuel efficient and more expensive. At one time, the car owner could perform routine maintenance on his car. This is no longer possible due to the complexity and compact designs of today.

Consider that in 1970 the average mileage for cars was about 8 mpg. Assuming an average vehicle miles per year of 12000, the gallons of gasoline used was 1500. At 20 mpg, for 12000 miles, 600 gallons of gasoline are consumed. At 30 mpg and 12000 miles, 400 gallons are needed. By increasing the fuel efficiencies of automobiles, the consumption of gasoline for the same number of miles driven was reduced by 60% at 20 mpg and 73% at 30 mpg.

A 54.5 mpg Corporate Average Fuel Economy (CAFÉ) fleet standard will make the cars so small that when there is an accident with a larger vehicle, there will be more fatalities. Air bags will not work when the small car is smashed into an accordion. In this instance the regulators have ignored science and forced political decisions. In their zeal to reduce emissions, they ignore common sense and have forgotten about cost/benefit analysis. The EPA claims huge fuel savings while potentially doubling the cost to build a car that can meet the 54.5 mileage standard. It should also be noted that as the fleet mpg requirement has been raised, more people are buying the larger SUVs and pickup trucks which have poorer mileage ratings. If Americans really wanted to drive small cars, the demand for SUVs and pickups would be very low. Maybe it is the government's objective to make autos so costly that no one will buy them and everyone will have to use mass transit if it is available. The use of this CAFÉ standard has progressed to the point that it is an abuse of power and control using government force.

Using science, a decision was made to use oxygenates in motor fuel to reduce smog. The choice to use ethanol derived from corn was a political decision. The unintended consequence of this is that ethanol usage has driven up the price of corn and caused inflationary pressure on the American family's grocery bill. Ethanol while good for reducing smog pollution is a bad gasoline blending component. It increases fuel handling costs because it must be handled separately from the oil portion of the gasoline. Ethanol is not as efficient a fuel as regular gasoline, delivering fewer vehicle miles per gallon. It absorbs enough water from the air when left standing for a long period to render a gasoline engine inoperable. If the EPA gets its way and forces 15% ethanol blending, it has been reported that this concentration will cause damage to older car engines. This is another case in which politics has really ignored science and will cause problems. A much better oxygenate blending component would be butanol. It does not absorb water like ethanol, can be blended and transported with gasoline by pipeline lowering handling costs and it has a higher octane rating giving the motorist better mileage. Ethanol motor fuel use is a case of political power and control using government force to implement poor science. Without a government subsidy, ethanol in gasoline is not economically sound.

This same logic can be used with respect to the sulfur content in our fuels. The sulfur in fuel when burned produces sulfur dioxide which at high concentrations can cause respiratory problems. Reducing the sulfur content in fuels from say 1% (10000 parts per million) to 50 parts per million makes sense because this represents a reduction of more than 99%. Reducing the sulfur content from 50 parts per million to 5 parts per million is also a 90% reduction, but what sense does it make to do this when from an emissions standpoint 99% of the sulfur has already been removed. When does regulation stop and common sense prevail?

Assuming that no improvements were made in treating exhaust emissions—which is not true—the emissions were reduced by 60% as average car mileage reached 20 mpg and 73% at 30 mpg. For older people, the better air quality is evident. In locations where once during a sunny day only a gray sky was visible, now there is a blue sky. When does good become good enough? The way I see it, now is the time to stop increasing auto gas mileage and see what effect it has on the environment and the economy.

It is interesting to note that significant changes are being made in the energy area. Hydraulic fracturing of shale oil has increased the United State's production of oil and natural gas, creating a surplus of natural gas. Surplus natural gas has lowered the cost to the point that long distance truckers can reduce their fuel costs by burning compressed natural gas instead of diesel. This has started a movement to build compressed natural gas engines and compressed natural gas fueling stations. When enough of these stations have been built, this may create a demand for cars to be powered using compressed natural gas.

It should be noted that dual fuel vehicles are available and a version has been used in other countries for many years. Vehicles that burn compressed natural gas (CNG) or gasoline are available. Other dual fuel combinations have also become available. Since two separate vehicle fuel gas tanks are needed, the available space within the vehicle may be reduced. Conversion kits for existing cars were available in the past. For those homes which use natural gas for heating and cooking, a natural gas compressor can be installed in the home to compress the natural gas used in the car.

Electric cars have been on the market for several years, but sales must be subsidized by the government and thus far the American public has resisted buying them. Most vehicles have a range of less than 100 miles and most of them require hours to recharge. The battery technology has not been developed sufficiently enough to produce cars with a typical 300 mile per charge range and there have been instances in which the battery has malfunctioned and caused the car to catch on fire. While the vehicle itself reports high mile per gallon equivalent (MPGe), this ignores the fact that the power used was probably generated by a power plant with a fuel efficiency of 40-50% with electric transmission losses of another 2 per cent and an electric motor efficiency of 80-90 per cent. In spite of this, the overall efficiency of an electric car does exceed that of a gasoline engine vehicle.

As long as science and common sense were used to determine where regulation is needed, generally the result has been good. Unfortunately, the EPA appears to have abandoned those principles in their regulatory world and has introduced political solutions instead. This is not good.

## Climate Change

Climate change caused by mankind was considered to be a possibility until it became known that so called scientists were manipulating data to falsely show climate change in order to get government grant money. To them, the money was more important than dedication to true science. After that disclosure, in my opinion, climate change became junk science and will remain junk science for years. It will take many many years of true and honest reporting on climate before anyone should even consider climate change to be a possibility. Climate change recommendations made without disclosing the raw data used to reach any conclusions are highly suspect. Conversely, mountains of raw data that are intended to overload the reader are most likely to also be suspect and meant to deliberately cause confusion. Such tactics are not science but politics. Climate change is the way by which politically connected special interest organizations will try to enrich themselves at taxpayer expense.

We simply do not know what effect, if any, is due to increased carbon dioxide in the atmosphere especially when that content is about 300 parts per million (ppm). How can a gas which is 300 ppm of the total atmosphere have such a strong effect on the world's climate? Carbon dioxide is a necessary part of the earth's ecosystem, but it has been labeled as a pollutant. Since carbon dioxide is heavier than air, it would be expected to stay closer to the earth's surface where it can be consumed by the plants and algae that produce the oxygen we need to live. Since all animal life uses oxygen and produces carbon dioxide, are the world governments trying to tell humanity that there are too many animals and they are ready to start killing us off? Has anyone considered how much carbon dioxide increase might be due to deforestation? With billions of trees being cut down, could any carbon dioxide increase—good or bad—be due more to this event than burning fossil fuels?

Water vapor is also a greenhouse gas and it is everywhere. Anecdotal reports are that the EPA is considering ways to try to control atmospheric water vapor. Since water covers about 70% of the earth's surface and the atmosphere routinely contains 1-5% (10,000-50,000 ppm) water vapor, it makes one wonder how the EPA will control the water vapor content. Maybe this is some EPA attorney making scientific recommendations. Again, this reminds me of the Albert Einstein quote: "The difference between stupidity and genius is that genius has its limits". Maybe there are some people out there wanting to buy some used bridges.

The climate change agenda is about making money and gaining power and control to use government force.

## Wind Energy

Wind energy is a subsidized form of energy that has been proclaimed as a way to generate power and reduce hydrocarbon fuel use, but it has also been an eagle killer. Isn't it illegal to kill eagles? Where are the so called environmentalists on this one? Why is there no screen or other means required so that the large birds cannot fly into one of the blades and be killed?

In general, these wind farms are located far removed from the power consumers. Who is going to pay for the transmission lines to the consumer so that the power can be consumed? Expect this charge to show up soon on your monthly electric bill.

The wind turbines are programmed to shut down when the wind speed starts to turn the generator too fast. Is this effectively using this mode of power generation?

Where does the consumer power come from when there is no wind?

Any and all wind energy government subsidies must be eliminated.

## Solar Power

Solar power works fine as long as the sun is shining. The cost to produce solar panels has been high and solar power has been heavily subsidized by the government.

We know that solar panels need sunlight to generate electricity. From where does the consumer get power when there is no sunlight? One way would be to generate excess power during the daytime and store this energy in batteries. Of course, this would increase the solar generation cost. It would work for fixed installations such as homes, but there would be problems providing dependable power for general consumer consumption and mobile units.

It would be a good thing to have the environmental activists who insist on renewable energy be forced to use only renewable energy daily. This precludes using any oil, natural gas or hydrocarbon-generated electric power. Obviously since air transport uses fuels, the activists cannot fly in commercial or private airplanes or drive any vehicle that does not use 100% renewable fuel.

## Ultimate Power Source

As long as the EPA does not try to regulate water vapor, the ultimate vehicle is a fuel cell which uses hydrogen as a fuel to generate the electric power needed for an electric car. For homes, the fuel cell could be used to furnish electric power. To make the fuel, electricity generated by solar panels would be used to disassociate water into its oxygen and hydrogen components. The hydrogen will be compressed to fuel cell pressure requirements and stored in a fuel tank. The hydrogen reacts with atmospheric oxygen in the fuel cell to produce the electricity needed for home use or to run the electric motor that powers a vehicle. The fuel cell emission is water vapor.

Please note that both pure oxygen and hydrogen can be very dangerous to handle.

Hydrogen fuel cells have been reliably used for many years, but units large enough to furnish power to large cities have yet to be developed.

## Water Needs

Recently certain areas of the country have experienced drought. Without water, food for the people and corn to produce ethanol cannot be grown. It is presumed that all kinds of studies will be done with almost all of them emphasizing conservation and water use restrictions. Please note that it has been estimated that approximately half of the water in open-air reservoirs is lost to evaporation, so covered storage of some sort will be needed.

Another way to meet water needs is to use technology to produce the water needed and that technology exists today. We have all the water we will ever need from the water source that covers 70% of our planet---the oceans. Water desalination is existing technology. In the Middle East, this is how they meet their water needs. Water for the farmer and industrial needs could be produced at strategic locations near the oceans and then pumped via pipelines and/or trucked to the end user. Desalination plants located in states near the Gulf of Mexico and the Atlantic and Pacific Oceans could supply the entire nation with its supplemental water needs. Will it be expensive? Maybe, but cost estimates would be easy to do once the water demand has been determined.

The shale oil fracking energy revolution has increased the need for water since each well generally requires from 1-6 million gallons of water. Once production is established from a fracked well, the well production depletes more quickly than a traditional oil well. That being the case, to maintain production from each field more wells will need to be drilled and more water needed. It remains to be seen if refracking an existing well would be effective in maintaining production rates. While the energy industry uses large quantities of water, they still do not use nearly as much water as agriculture. Much of the frack water used is recovered when production starts and the fracking area is relatively small, so using water to frack shale oil does not present an environmental problem. Water used in fracking can and should be recycled. One state governor demonstrated the safety of frack water by drinking some.

Maybe it would be in the best interests of agriculture and the energy industry to form a water alliance. It seems to make sense that the best way to finance and run these water supply desalination plants would be for the end users to form cooperatives. Then as the owners and users, no government monies would be needed and the water production could be controlled more efficiently to meet demand. It would be the best way since we know that the government cannot run anything efficiently.

Since we are depleting our water aquifers too quickly, we need to start producing desalinated water **NOW**. The politicians will want to create water conservation agencies that will be run by unelected bureaucrats with an agenda. The last thing the public needs is another government boondoggle agency. Water for food production is not a luxury, it is an absolute necessity. No water—no food. What is so difficult about that to understand?

## Department of Energy

The Department of Energy was formed in 1977 to formulate a plan for the United States to become energy independent. It has failed to do this. If this country is to become energy independent, it will be due to the oil and gas industry and its fracking of shale oil deposits. This is being done despite the federal government attempts to restrict all oil and gas exploration. Due to the fallacy of carbon dioxide emissions being destructive, political decisions drive this agenda instead of good science.

One smart thing the Department of Energy did do was to create the Strategic Petroleum Reserve which makes available crude oil for processing in an emergency. While it does cost money to maintain this crude oil storage, it is in the nation's best interest to keep it a viable option.

## Nuclear Power

At one time, nuclear power was to be the wave of the future. With accidents at Three Mile Island and Chernobyl, nuclear power became a pariah. These incidents were reinforced by the damage done to Japan's Fukushima nuclear facility from the recent earthquake and tsunami. Properly designed and located in relatively safe locations, they still can be a reasonable way to provide power for the world's economies. Please note that hindsight is always 100% correct and it is very easy to criticize decisions made previously.

One major problem is nuclear waste, which is now stored instead of being reprocessed to recover usable nuclear material.

Instead of wasting taxpayer monies on renewable energy companies, monies should be spent on renewable energy research and nuclear waste processing research so the specter of huge piles of radioactive material being stored for hundreds of years can be eliminated. Once again, politics triumphs over science to the detriment of everyone. If nuclear power is such a bad thing, why does the United States still use nuclear power in their submarines and aircraft carriers?

CHAPTER **9**

# Questionable Federal, State and Local Political Decisions and Regulations

## Incandescent Light Bulbs
Who was the genius that decided it was illegal for the normal incandescent light bulb to be manufactured and sold in the United States? The same light bulbs that have been used for over 100 years are now prohibited in order to save energy. Instead the new light bulb which contains mercury has to be used. When you dispose of the new light bulb, it is hazardous waste.

## Environmental Waste Disposal
To me, it is uncertain if anyone knows for sure what the specific geology of the earth is in sufficient detail at 5000-10000 feet below the earth's surface for miles in all directions, so I have a personal prejudice against the environmental practice of hazardous waste disposal into injection wells.

## Federal Lands
The federal government currently owns about 30% of the land mass of the United States. Why is the federal government controlling so much land and buying more land in primarily the western states? Could it be so that human use will be outlawed and the territory turned over to wildlife as advocates of Agenda 21 want to do? Does this agree with the premise that government works for the people?

Wouldn't it make more sense for the government to be selling the land, but ONLY to United States' citizens? You decide.

## Indian Affairs

The federal government has for years mismanaged this department. For the Department of Indian Affairs, the government needs to make a block grant to each tribe and then leave the Indians to govern themselves. Without dependency, it will reduce the incidence of poverty and alcoholism. Let them function as the independent communities they can be. For some tribes, the establishment of gambling has brought prosperity and improved living conditions. It should be the individual tribe's decision on how they wish to run their lives so long as they do not harm others—which I doubt would happen.

## Veterans Administration

For years the bureaucrats in the Veterans Administration (VA) have had a backlog of cases. Why can't this group do their work in a timely manner? The reason is that it is run by the federal government bureaucrats whose sole goal is to protect their jobs.

Another issue is troublesome. If the VA is doing their best to help veterans and their families, why is there a need for organizations such as the Wounded Warrior Project (WWP)? If the government is going to send young men and women to all parts of the world and have them fight to protect our freedoms, then why when these people are injured performing their duties doesn't the government take care of them? The government says they will, but they never do to the extent that is necessary. Some of these people are disabled for life. They need to be supported emotionally and financially to the extent necessary to ensure that their service was not in vain. The government is not qualified to do this task. Bureaucrats are empire builders—not public servants. Their only objective is to increase their power and control by expanding their departments to benefit themselves.

## Human Waste Disposal

Cities have for years been collecting and treating human waste. They aerate and use chemicals to treat the waste stream prior to discharging the treated liquid portion into a nearby river or stream. Periodically the residual solid waste is removed to be incinerated, maybe sent to a landfill or possibly used as a fertilizer as long as it is not used to grow crops consumed by people.

Rural areas have for years used septic tanks and drain fields to dispose of human waste. This type of disposal can present a problem with porous soils that might allow bacteria and viruses to leach into the drinking water supply. Septic drain fields do not work for clay soils, so an aerobic system was developed. Aerobic treatment is a permanent solution to treating human waste and is as good or better than municipal waste treatment. Municipal waste treatment plants have to deal with all kinds of materials and liquids that are dumped into the municipal sewer system that should never be sent to a residential or industrial aerobic treatment system. A home or business with an aerobic waste treatment system is a permanent waste treatment solution not a temporary one to later be replaced by a municipal treatment system.

# CHAPTER 10

# An American Manifesto for a Pendulum Nation

For a nation that swings from one extreme to the other when it should stop in the middle.

## Fair and Honest Elections

The United States will never have fair and honest elections as long as lobbyists and rich donors can in effect buy the politicians. Money is not the root of all evil, but it is the professional politician's best friend. Americans need to decide whether honest elections are worth paying for. I maintain that they are worth it.

To avoid voter fraud, only those persons registered to vote two weeks prior to the election should be allowed to vote after presenting a photo ID. Voters who want to vote but did not register two weeks prior to the election can be allowed to vote after being photographed and fingerprinted prior to being given a ballot and a voter ID card. Anything else is quite simply an open invitation to voter fraud.

The election officials must be responsible to ensure a fair and honest election. Anecdotal information is that it is easy to rig a voting machine by changing only two words of code and this information has been given to the Congress during testimony. Nothing has been done. To correct this, after each election, these machines must be impounded and kept under armed guard until it has been determined that the election was conducted honestly. An independent bonded inspector must inspect each machine for fraudulent programming before the election results are announced. Any other way to vote must also be impounded after the polls close. The penalty for voter fraud should be a minimum of ten years in prison for a first offence and a $10,000 fine. Should the public and election officials decline to pay election costs and not impound the votes, then they will have met Albert Einstein's definition of insanity: "Insanity: doing the same thing over and over again and expecting different results."

## Election Reform

Another way to reduce the need for money is for the government to give each person running for office in the *general election* an amount equal to one dollar per voter with a maximum of three persons running for any one office. These three persons would be decided by the voters during primary elections. Presumably using today's political party labeling these parties would be the Democratic, Republican and Libertarian/Independent parties.

The person running for office must raise money for his primary election with a maximum spending limit of one dollar per registered voter. All politicians will state that this is not enough money, but the idea is for them to get out and meet the voters and to use their brains to control expenses instead of begging rich donors who will later "own" them. Worse still would be to ask bundlers for money in which case the bundler will "own" the elected official. The penalty for not staying below the allowable amount is immediate disqualification and disqualification must be enforced even if the person is elected. We must eliminate persons with large fortunes buying a political office.

Maybe a better idea to save the taxpayer's money might be for all parties to run in the same primary election and have the three highest vote getters then proceed to the general election ballot.

There will be a limit of total time one can spend in elected office encompassing all levels of government. The person must decide for which office he or she will run. The maximum number of terms in local and state governments will be limited to two. Thus if someone runs for local office, then state office and finally a federal office, that person can serve only four terms---two federal and two state or local. Professional politicians have completely messed up the political system.

## Recall Elections

Every elected and appointed government official shall be subject to a recall by the voters and provision should be made to have election law changed to accommodate this necessary option. This is a very messy but necessary requirement in order for the people to maintain control over their government. This recall option must apply to everyone including the President of the United States, the Congress and the federal judiciary.

With initiation of the recall process by the voters, maybe the Congress will wake up and use their constitutional impeachment powers instead of going through the expense of a recall election.

## Political Action Committees

When a Political Action Committee (PAC) tells a lie in an ad and the lie can be proven, then the originator must retract that lie to the same distribution as the false claim. Failure to do so within two days makes the originator subject to a defamation lawsuit for an amount equal to ten times the cost for the original distribution. Failure to pay any defamation costs cannot be discharged by bankruptcy or dissolution of the PAC. As soon as the truth of the ad is challenged, the PAC must place into an escrow account an amount equal to ten times the original cost. Propaganda has no place in a political election.

## Federal Office Restrictions

The problem is money, and professional politicians are continual-
ly asking for money to get re-elected. Now if we limit the number
to times a politician can get elected, then we reduce their need for
money. Limiting each elected official to one term might not be a good
idea because it might eliminate good public servants, so for Congress,
a two term maximum would seem to be a good guideline. By limiting
the number of times a politician can run, we reduce their need for
money.

Another restriction is that all government pensions must be converted
to 401k equivalent. The maximum government contribution to each
401k is 5% of that office's annual salary. All special retirement and
health plans are prohibited—no exceptions.

## Federal Judiciary

All federal judges should be elected or, if appointed, shall retire after
having served a maximum term of ten years. All retired and/or federal
judges who have served for ten years are prohibited from adjudicat-
ing any court business.

Another restriction is that all government pensions must be converted
to 401k equivalent. The maximum government contribution to each
401k is 5% of that office's annual salary. All special retirement and
health plans are prohibited—no exceptions.

## State and Local Offices Restrictions

There should be a two term limit. Professional politicians after more
than two terms get to thinking that they own their office. Politicians
are like clothes, they must be changed frequently to stay clean.

Another restriction is that all government pensions must be converted
to 401k equivalent. The maximum government contribution to each

401k is 5% of that office's annual salary. All special retirement and health plans are prohibited—no exceptions.

## Non-elected Government Appointments

All government employees must pass a competency test before they can be appointed to a government job in the field which they are supposed to regulate. You do not appoint an attorney to a position that requires years of scientific technical experience. In lieu of that test requirement, the appointee must have demonstrated expertise for a minimum of ten years in the field that is to be regulated. Recent events have clearly demonstrated political appointments do not serve the public and the Peter Principle reigns supreme.

All government employees shall be limited to a 10-year term of service. There shall be no lifetime government positions. The exception to this length of service rule shall be those who require special training and who risk their lives in the performance of their duties. These persons are the military, law enforcement and fire fighting personnel. Their terms of service are limited to twenty years. In recognition of this type of service, each non-management employee at risk shall be provided with a government supplied life insurance policy and a disability insurance policy. To eliminate corruption and mismanagement, all such policies will be provided by an independent insurance company. This is especially important for the disability policies since the government has demonstrated that waste and fraud have historically gone unpunished. An independent insurance company in its own self interest will do its best to investigate and prevent fraud.

All government pensions must be converted to 401k equivalent. The maximum government contribution to each 401k is 5% of that office's annual salary. All special retirement and health plans are prohibited—no exceptions.

## Former Government Employees

All retired government employees will have a lifetime or ten-year prohibition from seeking employment or consulting with any entity that
is pursuing or currently does business with the government. We cannot have foxes guarding the hen house.

## Sunset Law Provision

Outdated and now useless laws most likely cause some violation of
law by every citizen every day. Laws that were issued many years ago
no longer apply. Therefore, it is proposed that every law issued have a
sunset date upon which it expires. This would clean up our laws and
regulations so that only those relevant would still apply. The Congress
and Federal executive departments must review all previous laws to
see if they still apply within twenty years.

## Regulation Rules

Coincidently, the problem with regulation is that in order to preserve
their jobs, the regulators keep issuing regulations that go beyond
common sense and create wasteful regulations. The stupidest regulation always costs money after being issued. The more companies
and people affected by this regulation, the more money that will be
wasted. Instead of money going into improvements, it will be spent
on reading and rereading the regulation to determine if and how it
affects the reader.

All regulations proposed must include a cost/benefit analysis and a
sunset date on which it expires. Included in this cost/benefit analysis
must be an estimate of the number of persons/entities affected and
a minimum cost of one hour per page at the prevailing dollar per
hour cost just to read the new regulation. All regulations issued incur
this cost. When the estimated cost of the regulation has been issued,
if the actual cost exceeds the estimated cost by 15%, that department is issued a warning. A second issued regulation that exceeds
the estimated cost incurs a penalty of 10% of the current department

budget which will be implemented for the following year's budget. A third issued regulation that exceeds the estimated cost requires that the department head and those regulators involved be terminated. Good regulations solve problems and bad regulations only waste everyone's time and money.

## Balanced Budget Amendment

It is time that citizens of this country stop listening to professional politicians and start thinking for themselves. If you don't have the money to go to a restaurant, you don't go. You don't buy that new car or house if you do not have the money. Many states have constitutional requirements that their budgets must balance every year and they do just fine. It is time that the federal government follows the states' lead and adopts a balanced budget amendment.

## Repeal the Seventeenth Amendment

Repeal the seventeenth amendment and return to the selection of senators by each state's legislature. The direct election of senators by the electorate now is a glorified representative election where the most money available for campaigning wins too many times. While the selection of a senator by the state legislature is political, the senator has an obligation to represent that state's best interest instead of his own and that of his political party. When the senator does not follow his state's direction, the senator is removed from office.